TRUMPELSTILTSKIN

By

Way of the Brothers Grimm

inherit books
nyc 2016

ISBN 978-0-9833472-2-4

TRUMPELSTILTSKIN

TRUMPELSTILTSKIN

A poor and disenfranchised man had a beautiful daughter. One day he went to the king and said, "I have a daughter who can turn straw into gold."

The king said, "She sounds like the kind of girl I hire. Send her to my palace tomorrow."

Bed of Straw

When the girl arrived at the palace, the king took her to a small room in one of the towers. In the middle of the room was a straw bed.

"Tonight, you're going to turn this straw bed into gold. It'll be greater than anything you've ever done. Very great."

The beautiful girl sat on the straw bed. She didn't know what to do. That night, she cried herself to sleep. Then, in the total darkness of the room, she was awakened by an "odd little fellow."

"What are you crying about?" said a voice.

"Alas," answered the girl, "I'm supposed to turn this straw bed into gold, and I don't know how to do it."

"I'm going to help you with that," boasted the voice.

She couldn't see the little fellow in the dark, but from what she could tell he seemed quite small indeed.

"I doubt that," said the beautiful girl.

The night passed. . . .

It turned out not to be a golden experience at all. In fact, it was a disaster. A complete disaster.

The next day the king moved the beautiful girl to a bigger room, with a bigger straw bed.

"Tonight," said the king, "you will turn this straw bed into gold, or" – his mouth formed an obscene hole – "YOU'RE FIRED!"

That night in the dark the little fellow woke her up again.

"Please go away," she cried.

"I'm not going away," he said, in a voice that sounded very much like the king's. "Everybody thinks I'm going away, but I'm never going away!"

Another night passed. . . .

But the experience this time was even less golden than before. Very bad.

"Help me escape!" said the girl to the odd little fellow. "I've been nice to you. But – you know – gold is hard to fake."

"If you can guess my name, I will," said the little fellow with an arrogant smirk. "But if you can't, I get to rule your life for the next four years. Do we have a deal?"

"What else can I do?" she said. "I'm trapped."

The next morning the king was in a wild disheveled state.

"I'm moving you to a suite," he announced.

Soon she was installed in a great apartment with a huge straw bed. On the walls were many portraits of the king. A large window overlooked the park.

"Tonight it's gold or . . . ." The king drew a knife-like finger across his throat, his hair shimmering and trembling with greedy desire.

That afternoon, when the Mexican maid came to clean the suite, the girl asked her if she knew the odd little fellow that was sometimes in the palace at night.

"I think I know who you mean," said the maid. "I've seen the king playing with him. He's tiny. Very small."

"Yes, "said the girl. "That's him exactly! Do you know his name?"

"The king calls him Trumpelstiltskin," said the maid.

KING'S TOWER PALACE

That night when the odd little fellow turned up in the girl's room she was ready for him.

"If I guess your name, I get to go free."

"Yes," said the little fellow. "Back to poverty and all the rest. But if you don't guess it, you're mine for four years – *and perhaps four more.*"

"It's not Jeb?"

"No!"

"Marco?"

"No!"

"Ted?"

"No!"

"Ben?"

"No!"

"John?"

"No!"

"How about . . . *Trumpelstiltskin?*"

Suddenly, the little fellow began to shrink. It was like watching an orange inch disappear right before your eyes. Then he was gone. In the next moment the door to the suite stood open. With a wild happiness the girl raced out of the palace and back into the bright sunlit world of the city, as if it had all been only a terrible, unthinkable dream.